America Today:
A Personal View

By

G K McGilvary

America Today:
A Personal View

Contents

Book Structure

The method chosen for this journey is rather unusual: first off, I have provided my thoughts, summaries and conclusions reached after many years. Only then have parallels been made with the course of my personal life and first contacts with Americana. It has been a liberating exercise; one that has allowed me to come to terms with the world here and now.

Take Care when Analysing America

One of the strangest things for a non-American English language speaker to grasp is the USA citizen's singularly different use of words (not to mention pronounciation of many.). 'Alien' is one of these. Being a Scot makes me an 'alien', i.e not one of them. I could be from Mars or Sirius, makes no difference. Yet for others in the world using the English language this American usage is bizarre in the extreme.

From clues presented by such curiosities in American speech and idiom, it becomes important to be wary and to approach the USA, its inhabitants and its culture very carefully. In other words, tt 'behoves one' to understand American phrases. [I will return to such curiosities later.]

With such thoughts in mind, I have tried to see America in some of its many manifestations as perceived by a 'Johnny Foreigner' such as myself, as my English cousins used to say, or it might have been P.G.Wodehouse!

You could say that if there are any messages contained herein, these are primarily aimed at myself, such has been the interest this country and its people have inspired; and because of a lifetime of contact and reflection.

This has resulted in a catch-as-catch-can of reminiscences and events dating from my earliest years. It has also meant a lot of analysis, of comparison and contrast, such as between North American and European cultures—and is enlivened at odd moments by a good-natured swipe at my own nearest and 'dearest' neighbour, the Englishman. Every attempt has been made to keep the tone light and to avoid a cold, impersonal study.

I have made a determined effort to find America, to locate its soul—and this has proved to be difficult, because America means and has meant different things to so many people.

For much of my formative life Hollywood was the dominant medium. At one level this meant accepting what Hollywood presented as a reasonable picture of life in the USA; on another plane, of interpreting and understanding underlying truths, myths and mysteries, tongue in the cheek representations, as well as grim facts and statistics no one wanted to tell, but which were sometimes exposed as the film strip unrolled.

As the 'real' USA began to impact, so Hollywood took more of a backseat—that said, it was (and is) always there—even as my perspective changed and continues to change to this day.

Surprising Self Discoveries

In writing this essay a lot of things have become clearer to me. For instance, I simply had no idea that the American way of life, despite its global penetration via films and now TV and the internet, had shaped me so much. I'm not really sure that this makes me exceptional. I am only too aware that the rest of the world finds it well-nigh impossible not to be influenced; but has America affected these others as much as it has me? Perhaps I am being naive.

A popular thriller writer of our time (who writes under the name 'Lee Child') and happens to be British, has created an American hero who displays his daring in an American setting. When asked if this had been easy to do he made it clear there could be no escape for the rest of us when it came to knowing what is or has happened in the USA.

Clearly there is a converse side to all this. It occurs in a question that I don't think I have seen answered very much: just how do ordinary Americans view the rest of the world? Does this ever really come up—on TV, or radio? Are everyday citizens even interested in what goes on other than between "sea and shining sea"?

In stark contrast to the past, I rather think that nowadays many do, even among the zillions who don't have a passport. The internet is everywhere: and what once was one way traffic— that is, of information pouring out of America, this has transmuted into a means of bringing the outside world into the lives of many lonely souls in the USA, even to Nebraskans!!

Let me return, for a moment, to how much America has shaped the real me. Certainly, neither English nor Continental influences seem to have figured in my early make-up—literature shared with the English, Irish and Welsh and aspects of European culture I subsumed latterly. (These I come to, in a bit).

Still on this theme, I am also sure that it has been the distinctive nature of Scots, Irish and Welsh cultures that have saved them from the Southern English bias that pours forth from a London-controlled media. This sort of 'dig in your heels' attitude has conditioned the 'Celtic fringe' to retain the strongest feelings for their own small pieces of the earth. It all kind of takes me back to The Stamp Act and all the shenanigans of the 1760s and 1770s along the eastern seaboard of the American continent.

A major aspect of this self-scrutiny has been the question I have set myself to explain: just what do I mean by 'America' and what do I mean by 'Scotland? My thoughts run parallel to those of a late friend, Dr. Angus Calder, who in his book, published in 2002, set about analysing 'Scotlands of the Mind'. There are and have been many 'Scotlands'—as his work demonstrates. There are also, and have ever been, many 'Americas'—as numerous books and films make clear. 'Nature and nurture'—to use the present phrase employed to indicate what constitutes an individual's 'ingredients'—ensure this is so.

Within the shepherding influence of what always reduces to a handful of major shaping events, people carry on with their lives, conducting themselves according to the customs of their peers and (as far is allowed within each political entity) along with personal inclinations.

With the USA, these shaping events might be seen as the American Declaration of Independence, the Constitution and the First Amendment, the Civil War, the ambitions of a clutch of Presidents: Washington, Lincoln and FDR in particular; and of significant inventions, discoveries and shifts in world power.

Naturally, people belonging to the world of academe, of agriculture and business, of religion, militarism and so on, will define an American world slightly different from that of the other.

The down-and-out obviously experience a different America from those with sufficient funds for a decent life; and they in turn from that of the mega-rich.

Particular Themes

I have been quietly impressed by the legacy of the early (and of the continuing) Scottish—American connection: of the Presidents, the Constitution, early education, industrial leaders, like Carnegie; golf, clan associations, whisky, tartan and shortbread, hill-billy music and folklore. Many Scottish discoveries and inventions have been perfected by Americans—although one of your own smart-speaking, funny men, 'Rich' in words as well as name, has described our whisky as being ruined by his fellow-countrymen—not left to be enjoyed as a pure malt or even a blend!!

There are many, many differences, obviously: getting back to the language we share, English, but don't understand each other: Cookies and biscuits, for example. Spelling is another thing: 'favour' and 'favor'; 'cheque' and 'check'; how we pronounce route (ourselves: 'root'; Americans 'rouwt'); humans become 'yumans'; tune becomes 'toon'; 'maths' becomes 'math'.

It's just great. Other differences: there are so few bus stops; nobody walks. Your police (with their guns) are so different. In this dangerous age, and with massacres and shootings every other day, the right of Americans to have a gun seems to me to be unsustainable; to others it justifies the right to do so. There is no winner.

More differences: Grid-iron and baseball are both 'World Series': what does that mean? Apart from some Japanese involvement in recent times, it just seems to mean the US. The number of churches—especially Baptist—is eye-boggling.

The 'quaintness' of school buses sticks in the mind. Train stations are like palaces; the loud public conversation. It's good to know Americans shout the same in the US as they do abroad. To many a foreigner it is dfficult to understand the flag flying that goes on everywhere, on every building, public and private.

On a local basis, the eco-friendliness of the average American is to be admired, preserving the trees, for example; the pressure brought to bear upon National Parks to conserve the mighty wilderness. (Hurrah for the man from Dunbar, Scotland).

Such laudable comment cannot be heaped upon American business people and politicians, who will still not agree to talks aimed at curbing carbon dioxide emission. We Brits are not much better, but we are trying. The US government, the Chinese, Asians and others pouring out this filth that will end all our lives, should be ashamed. Nor is it credible that the richest nation on earth still has no free health care system in place—and, yes, I have heard all the arguments put up against this.

It is also excruciating, the amount of 'back-scratching', and 'log rolling' (as these manoeuvres are called) that goes on in American politics; side by side with lobbying by some of the most powerful industrialists on earth; and the dubious manner (at least to the rest of the world) in which some elections are run. In the opinion of many, the USA has not always brought forth the quality of leader in the White House that it needs and expects, because of how the party system is run and the blatant use of personal wealth.

The bureaucracy and illegal immigration faced are inter-mingled: the latter savagely increasing the need for even more of the former. Whether the States will be able to reduce the officialdom that threatens to engulf everything, however, I'm not sure.

Entering via airports and shipping terminals anywhere in the world is a nightmare: After standing in line in one place comes the order, 'Take your shoes and belt off, sir, and deposit all metalic objects in the basket'. On to another line: This time the order is 'put your index finger here, please—and look straight into the camera lens.' If headed for America, don't dare say you haven't a visa, ESTA form, customs declaration, or an up-to-date passport.

The spoof request made to Armstrong and company, the first men on the moon, on re-entry, that they fill-in immigration forms, says it all. That said, it is no joke in south-western USA. The massive cross-border invasion from the Mexico side is so bad it appears to be threatening the whole economic and cultural nature of the borderland on the US side—something that has already had political ramifications.

How American do You want to Be?

Well, I must say the obvious—that I'm more than grateful for the good things that America has already given me, and I can't wait for more: the dream of a better life, the writers, the films, the music, the technology; to continue to learn and to imitate, the eagerness to 'turn a buck'. Yet, apart from what amounts to a relatively few items, I see nothing to really excite me nowadays; which means I am probably better remaining just as I am.

In the world of sport, it might be that American golf, athletics and swimming will continue to contribute something to the larger world. Baseball, basketball and American football leave me flat—mind you, so does much of the jumped up football (soccer) offered here.

American TV is even worse—it seems to me—than the British variety, mainly because of the never-ending adverts. The sad fact is, the content for so many programmes in Scotland, (especially for those of juvenile age) come mainly from the US; hough I think we still have some decent offerings of our own for the very young. Some series, I hope, will be banned from the screen. However, given how cheap it is to produce digital characters, and cartoon versions of talking animals, real or cuddly imitations—all yapping at me—I realise this is a forlorn hope.

On a more serious note, there is little doubt that my own brand of national consciousness that has kept me in Scotland will continue to do so. When all is said and done, love of the good people you know, the feel of the land and of the sea that surrounds 'Auld Scotla', are in my bones—I can't visualise belonging anywhere else.

Sure, I hate the spurious nationalism that is all around; what I have is a quiet satisfaction regarding who I am and pride in the forces that have nurtured me. I feel government should be shaped by people who are near, who share in the environment and know the needs of those they live among—the closer to home the better.

It is not right that rules are made by strangers from hundreds of miles away, whose policies and platforms must incorporate a larger entity. Noticing the same feeling among those of other nations for their homeland makes me feel this is natural to mankind.

So thank goodness for America that over the centuries she has been able to take and rebuild the lives of so many lost souls who had this right kept away from them in the lands of their birth. [It is also obvious, from the above that I am a believer in 'States Rights' against the ever-increasing and overbearing grasp of Federal control.]

Fears

If there is a fear in me regarding America's future it is in the power being invested in her various internal security forces: FBI, CIA, Homeland Security and so on. What is tmost errifying is the display of sheer untouchability among such forces, especially if the crude reality is really that portrayed in countless films and books. This is especially intimidating when linked with 'Spy in the Sky' global scrutiny, pressure groups being bank-rolled by owners of military-industrial complexes and financial gurus.

The whole package of present day America appears to be backed by a legal system only the rich can afford, screwed to the maximum; also one always biased to defending the homeland, and seemingly able to bring about any verdict desired.

The tendency among so many with vested powers to see everything only in black or white terms (and this is meant literally as well as figuratively) and to lock away forever those deemed hostile, whether or not a crime has been committed, attacks the whole existence of a civilized democratic life. When a small group of people can exert such control, despite the political safeguards that once meant so much, then the USA and the world must be on guard.

This point about the law in the USA needs stressing. America is, quite properly, a land that lives under the rule of law; but like a great many countries, this law has become unaffordable to the many, and (to the eyes of an outsider) is being abused. It would appear that the power of the American legal profession is almost unassailable—and that it has become well-nigh impossible to cleanse the quango-like arrangements in America that seem to exist between the forces of the law, the penal authorities, security agents and police forces.

Additionally, though I know it won't happen, because it is so ingrained, if only the self-view of moral superiority that appears in so many American speeches, songs and prayers could end, the other peoples on earth would look at her in the light in which she wants to be perceived. I am sure Americans know that every nation that exists also prefixes its name with "God bless..."

Danger from Abroad
Apart from climate change, continuing widespread ignorance and superstition, the immediate enemy would appear to be Islamic fundamentalism, and the drive for world domination that fills the minds of the deadly terrorist groups this creed seems to breed. All fair-minded people must be horrified at the sickening carnage they inflict.

Unfortunately, many of the Christian Right (and not just in America) diametrically (and correctly) opposed to the views of such people, would appear to have a similar in-built stance of: 'we are right and they are wrong'. That and the nonsense of 'intelligent design' have to be shown for what they are, and rooted out.

That said, the American presence is needed now everywhere in the world, just as much as it was during both World Wars.

However, she should stay out of things as much as she can—stop seeing US interests involved in every skirmish, world-wide.

She must limit her 'world policeman' role; do something about the spying on others that is going on by agencies like the NSA (even long-time friends being mistreated); reign in the power of her mega-rich; and reduce the influence of military-industrial lobbying, especially regarding foreign affairs.

Final Words

I still see the United States of America as the best chance for man's survival. The US gives hope for the future in my eyes, though I admit, I have been biased since childhood; (those Hollywood movies, I guess).

I see America's greatness in the technology that is being advanced there, especially in the Universities and Science Institutes; in the massive investments undertaken; in the 'lets just do it' attitude, instead of interminable talk.

However, the internet has to be taken out of private hands: the power of the likes of Google, Yahoo, Amazon and Apple is frightening.

American music and literature will continue to excel, of that I am sure. [But what happened to American art, along the way? Apart from a few exceptional people like Benjamin West, Whistler, Norman Rockwell, Jackson Pollock, Epstein, and perhaps Audubon and Andy Warhol, where are the artists and their work?]

Is this merely a case of ability and fame in the US not being recognised in Europe—or (as applies to many) of a joint claim: the artists being born somewhere in Europe, or elsewhere, before turning up later, in America?

Space must not become a theatre of war for fighting and feuding by the human animal that for now, rules this earth. Peaceful exploration and understanding of the Cosmos sustains all our hopes for the future of mankind.

The space exploration must continue to embrace everyone, using America's remarkable know-how. The rivalry with Russia, China, and no doubt, sooner or later, with India, will continue; but hopefully it will remain friendly. So much is dependent on global models; and co-existence is absolutely necessary, whether in money, goods or anything else.

America is magnificent in all its manifestations: so attractive, such a huge, lived in sort of a place. It is always attention-grabbing, exciting; and its people are as interested in you, as you are in them. I wish it and its people well.

♦♦♦

Personal Connection with America

In the Beginning – Films

My earliest recollection of the word 'America' was probably when I was about four years old (1943)—the middle of the 2nd World War. Mum and dad were talking about 'America becoming involved—though I didn't know any 'America' and didn't understand who or what he she or it was involved with, or what he she or it was involved in.

Another memory— now about six years old—of smashing films: Westerns, with Tom Mix, Gene Autry, Hopalong Cassidy (my favourite) and his horse, Topper; Boris Karloff and Lon Chaney in all sorts of horror films.

Mid-day matinees on a Saturday where, at the end of the film the hero was hanging by his finger-tips from a cliff, and we were told to return next week to see what happened—i.e. the original "cliff hanger".

Then there were Laurel and Hardy, Chaplin, Ben Turpin, Harold Lloyd—and the guy with the dead-pan face, Buster Keaton—all of them marvellous. I saw every one.

It cost two, 2lb jam jars, to enter the village cinema for the First House of the evening. (Cinema was not the right word for the Welfare Hall; it was more commonly referred to as 'Billy's Bug House').

Two of our very scarce pennies paid for the late evening performance. Oh, how I loved these films; and then, when colour came some years later and John Wayne strutted about, surrounded by the beauty of Arizona—'wow, that was something else'—as we learned to say.

We became good at copying a speech that was so new to us. 'The Wizard of Oz'; Disney's 'Fantasia' and 'Snow White'; 'Gone with the Wind'—yes, this was America; and I don't think my juvenile view of what was the real United States of America—courtesy of Hollywood— ever really changed. Well, maybe it has—a little.

Wasn't it strange that all this adoration was not that of a kid actually living in the United States, it was taking place thousands of miles away from America. I and my comrades lived in the scattered villages that populated 'the badlands' of Scotland's central belt; among the slag-heaps, surrounded by the pock-marked landscape of the coalfields.

We young ruffians would imitate our heroes, like Jimmy Cagney with his rapid-fire speech: 'You dirty rat, bang, bang.' (I know, I know, he didn't really say it). Pat O'Brian's tired-faced detective and his equally rapid-fire returns made us goggle then imitate. Did people really talk like that, we wondered?

It would have made no difference where we kids lived in Scotland, however, because American films and comics dominated everyone's imagination—adults as well. Cowboys and Indians, bows and arrows, tomahawks and Bowie knives; these vied with beautiful chorus girls, and brassy, gum-chewing 'broads'. This tidal wave of American culture made certain that scenarios, such as the musicals these girls decorated—and the music that brought it all to life—would live in our hearts forever.

Why was this so, you may ask? It was a question easily answered by anyone you spoke to in Britain, during and immediately after the war. Britain had become just as dependent upon America, in a cultural sense, as she was in material things.

Sure, the Marshall Plan was probably the saving of us—even as young school kids some of us knew that—but it was the enriching picture of life in America, seen in these films, that enthralled. You should have seen mum's face when she first came across washing machines, and 'hoovers' that cleaned the floor—labour-saving devices of every kind. What an effect all that had!

Unquestionably, they talked funny, these Americans, but were easy to listen to and understand—more like us than these 'pesky' Continentals, who gabbled away, making some sort of noise we couldn't make out.

The connection was most definitely transatlantic; there were huge gulfs between us and the Europeans, more than just the language problem. Also, the fact that the Germans, who had been our enemies for so long, were Europeans was something that kept being presented to us in films, newspapers, classrooms and general chatter. They were still the foe in what remained of the 1940s and early 1950s.

Then there was another factor that came into play that favoured the Americans. They didn't particularly like the English either! We Scots knew who our traditional enemy was. Didn't we win at Bannockburn, show them how to play football (soccer) and beat them consistently.

It rankled that BBC radio (no TV then) consistently 'spoke down' to us in Received Pronounciation; in fact they did so to anyone who was not of the 'Home Counties' or a 'London gel'.We Scots were presented as of a sub-culture and always in some menial position. Similar to the 'provincial' English, who were shown in a servile light as well.

To many in power in Southern England, we had no class or breeding. A Scot was used to portray almost every scene of drunkenness. Had the English never understood the satire in the film 'Whisky Galore'?

Another good thing about 'The Yanks' was that they were having none of this 'class' stuff that dominated English life ('I know my place, Sur!')—and neither were we. 'Yankee Doodle Dandy' seemed to march quite happily alongside 'Wha' Dare Meddle Wi' Me'. We liked the Yanks because of this.

Start of a More Critical attitude towards Hollywood films

Those early films, I suppose, have laid down what is still the best representation of America in my mind: the cowboy on his horse, complete with Stetson and with pearl-handled colts on his belt; the movie 'Shane', the Marlboro advert, 'Hoppy and Topper' trouncing wrong-doers.

A later change in me—horror of horrors—was that I saw fit to question my beloved American film industry. That said, I can still defend Hollywood as having produced more pure entertainment than any other medium; and on the whole, despite all I have to say, still comes out on the plus side.

I think 'Brigadoon' set off my alarm system. What were they doing? Despite a couple of memorable tunes, it was crass stuff!

Then, Mary Queen of Scots was 'murdered' by Elizabeth and Lord Chancellor Burleigh in so many ways, I lost count.

Mary Queen of Scots

The (first) film about 'Greyfriars Bobby' passes muster. It's about the faithful little dog that slept on its master's grave every night until it also passed away. The dog's statue still stands outside the Kirk of the Greyfriars, in Edinburgh, where his master lies.

Greyfriars Bobby

They did better with RLS's 'Treasure Island' and 'Kidnapped', but a foul job with his 'Strange Case of Dr Jekyll and Mr Hyde'.

Robert Louis Stevenson

Also, it seems to have completely missed Americana that Sir Walter Scott's imagination provided the substance for countless 'sword, shield and buckler' type of presentations, like 'Ivanhoe'.

Ivanhoe

It seems to have avoided everyone that Arthur Conan Doyle's life in Edinburgh laid the basis for his Sherlock Holmes character

Sir Arthur Conan Doyle   Sherlock Holmes

It is a similar story with J M Barrie, who created 'Peter Pan, or the Boy who wouldn't Grow Up'.

J M Barrie

Perhaps I should be thankful that Hollywood eyes have not yet fallen upon the poet, Robert Burns! Or have they?

Robert Burns

Hollywood and Scotland

Another, almost unforgivable trait is the feeble perception by Hollywood moguls of what Scots have brought to the world. Despite since early modern times having been at the forefront of almost every field of endeavour in the political, commercial and industrial worlds; in discovery and the mapping of the earth; in engineering, inventiveness, medicine, education and botany.

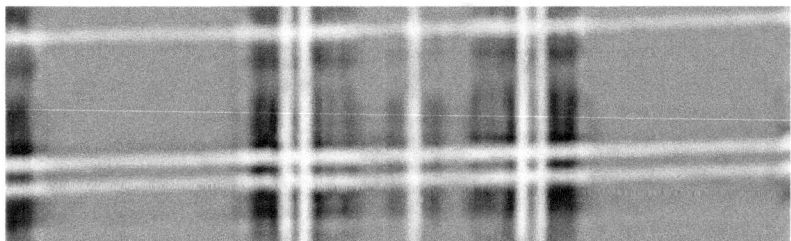

What is usually served is a re-hash of haggis, shortbread, tartan, kilts and bagpipes.

The unvarnished truth is that Scots (learning a great deal from others, and especially from the Dutch) developed professionalism in every major field from the 1680s onwards: such as in medicine, education and botany. This was long before the rest of the world was even aware of the word 'professional', far less the skills embraced.

The nearest to any form of recognition from American producers are the feats of Andrew Carnegie and that of 'Scotty' in 'Star Trek' (the one an industrialist, the other an engineer).

Andrew Carnegie

Have they never heard of that genius of the financial field, John Law; of the founding of New Orleans; or of Mackenzie and the North-West passage?

John Law of the Mississippi Scheme

What about Dr Livingstone - other than Stanley's: "Dr Livingstone, I presume".

Livingstone

When will they 'do' a production that appraises the Scottish Enlightenment—and of the impact this had on founding America?

Alexander Graham Bell was a Scot, although the telephone invention was made by him in America where he had settled.

Alexander Graham Bell

So was Pinkerton and his detective agency, who hailed from Glasgow. Protecting Presidents was one of his duties.

To me, the 'daddy of them all' (i.e. the best) was James Clerk Maxwell, who really laid the ground work for all future inventions in electricity, magnetism and optics. He inspired Einstein and was regarded as the middle man between Isaac Newton and himself.

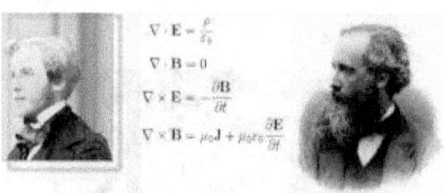

James Clerk Maxwell

What the above really says, readers, is that I had discovered who I really am. No longer was there a prism always in front of my eyes, directing my vision and thought through the projections of Hollywood, England, Europe or elsewhere.

In the words of yet another incredible Scot, Sir Patrick Geddes, I am now able to: 'Think global, act local'. I am a Scot.

Sir Patrick Geddes

Teens

In the teenage years of the 1950s, this love-affair with America continued and grew stronger. In our school atlases, we learned where America was; and of course, we all became aware that America had won the 2nd World War all by itself!! We had seen Audi Murphy do so (a real genuine hero, by the way) and countless other film stars, like Richard Widmark and, yes, Big John Wayne. We were also aware these film stars were carving out fabulous careers and making lumps of money while doing so—boy, the envy this instilled. Uncles and aunts, however, who during the war had rubbed shoulders with Americans in London (you couldn't find them anywhere else, only there and on American bases) informed us of how decent these real people were—and of their nylons, chewing gum and of the clothes they wore, better than anything you could find at home.

Then there was the music that was coming out of America. It was magical: the crooners—Crosby and Sinatra, Perry Como, Nat King Cole; the big dance bands, Artie Shaw, Benny Goodman and Glen Miller, whose death saddened us all. Swing, be-bop and JAZZ; 'heh, man, that Louis Armstrong was really somethin'. Ella Fitzgerald, her voice was just incredible—still is on CD. During my later teens, which were closely aligned with my introduction to girls and dance halls, the American influx just kept a comin': stars like Johnnie Ray, Kay Starr, Frankie Lane and Guy Mitchell kinda headed my list.

It was not really the same, however, with early motor cars. The 'Tin Lizzies' that Henry Ford's factories were pouring out were quite unfamiliar to us, as were all the others coming out of Detroit: the Packards, Buicks, Lincolns, and so on. We saw then in the many films depicting American family life; and they were integral to the lives of the city gangsters being portrayed in the movies. Like the detached homes and the city skyscrapers they inhabited, these were all unfamiliar.

Instead, we were driving our own wonderful cars: the Rovers, Bentleys (some hope!), Austins and Morrises.

My dad had managed to acquire a 1937 Rover (see above) a beautiful model, with running boards along the sides, doors that opened from the front, and a boot that was modelled with a wheel-shaped space to carry the spare. I passed my driving test in that car, but not before my old grandfather had knocked down a line of wall that belonged to the tallest men in Scotland — two brothers who almost reached the 8 foot mark!! Damage to the car? Well, nothing visible—she was made of solid stuff—only a bent track-rod end. Can't say the same about the wall!!

American mores were now completely familiar to us; and everyday American performers easily competed with the like of England'sTommy Handley. Mind you, he was stupendous in his own right, especially in the wonderful ITMA ('Its That Man Again') programme from London that we heard on the 'Cat's Whiskers' (battery radio).

American jokes and slang were much more welcome   and definitely more often heard in the streets— than 'Wullie' Shakespeare—though 'The Sonnets' and the major plays made a deeper impression than I cared to admit then.

The American shows also easily beat the Gilbert and Sullivan productions, like *The Mikado* that we were forced to watch (or participate in) at school. Funny, though, we never could speak with an authentic American voice—apart from 'stick 'em up' or 'reach for your gun'; kinda like Mel Gibson today trying on a Scottish brogue while being William Wallace, our national hero. [Okay, the English I know say I still can't speak their language properly.]
By this time, we adolescents understood better just how vital the American entry to the war had been: of Pearl Harbour and the truly brutal struggle against the Japanese: of Guadalcanal

and Mid-Way. Newspapers were full of the North Africa campaign, followed by the ferocious fighting around Salerno and Monte Cassino, then onwards through Italy.

Thankfully came the D-Day landings and the beginning of the end for the Nazis. It took a little longer for the Japanese surrender—but, of course, there was very little understanding regarding the fearsome weapon of war that ended things in the east. It soon became very clear, however, that the Atom bomb really signified the future of mankind.

Our comprehension of the films, of comics ('Superman' especially) of the music and magazines emanating from America, was now much more advanced. We had more perspective with advancing years; though this did not negate our appreciation of the heroic American effort (of civilians as well as the fighting men and women); and that their endeavours had worked to our benefit.

Now, however, we understood better what we too had accomplished; and also the tragic sacrifices made by the then USSR. The funny thing was that at that stage of life I had never ever seen a real live American, far less speak to one.

However, though all the splendid things continued to gush forth from that fabled land beyond the Atlantic, such as: the promise of success, and assurances of progress and achievement for all, it was getting a bit more complicated, and difficult to have a fixed viewpoint on things.

We had to work our way around Hiroshima and Nagasaki, evaluate the Cold War roles and the Berlin Airlift. It also became necessary to come to grips with a pivotal shift that had taken place in world affairs: the replacing of British, French and German overlordshhip with that of America and the USSR. It became imperative that we learning how these countries ruled them—and now us.

The checks and balances in the US system gained full marks: Separation of the Supreme Court from other branches, the Bill of Rights and the introduction of the 1st Amendment, all of this was excellent.

But, why were coloured people still being treated this way: the segregation, hangings and hate. An awful lot of them were killed and maimed during the war years, fighting for their country and for freedom; and still were—in every war that sprang up afterwards, from Korea onwards.

Yet a black man couldn't walk into the front lobby of a grand hotel back home. We 'aliens' (how I hate being pigeon-holed by this word) could only scratch our heads at this, being powerless to do anything about it; but to say we regretted what was happening would be false—we hated it. This was a side of the America that had saved us with her intervention in two wars, and which we cared for that we did not like.

Newsreels now told their own story of the sheer power of the American dollar and of US military might throughout the world; of Britain's humiliation over Suez, when America pulled a few strings.

Still, the US might have gone back into 'Splendid Isolation'. Instead, 'Old Joe' Stalin, until his death in 1954, knew what he was up against if he tried to muscle further west. It was a blow, nevertheless, that not even 'Uncle Sam' could prevent the atrocities of the Hungarian and then the Czechoslovakian uprisings, or help out.

Towards the end of the 1950s, there is litle doubt that the nuclear presence at Faslane, on the Holy Loch, sitting on the outskirts of Glasgow, when combined with the rise of CND, soured further our regard for America's leaders.

Nobody likes the idea of being a target for hostile forces to aim at; and with a population of millions on the doorstep it began to be asked whether the American military were more concerned with their own far-flung security than the support they had experienced from these 'cute' people in 'Scatland'. It is still a very live issue—the submarines, with their lethal warheads are still there.

The Young Man

From 1957 to the end of 1962, I saw service in the Royal Air Force and was posted all over England and abroad; but still no US citizen crossed my path. The nearest I came—something I remember very clearly (still got the snaps)—was of sitting beside the wreck of an American Landing Craft on the island of Masirah, which lies just at the entry to the Persian Gulf. [That's me, extreme left.]

Everywhere I went in the Near-East and Kenya there were plenty of white people: Britons, Kenyans, Rhodesians, South Africans, Australians and Europeans, as well as the whole black and coloured populations of Africa, Asia (India especially) and Arabia—but where were the Americans to fuss and gush over. There was no one to talk with about Norman Mailer, or about the fate of the 'Okies' that Steinback had let us glimpse in 'Grapes of Wrath'. I wanted to ramble on about Bix Beiderbecke, Buddy Holly and the Crickets; about Country and Western music, Blue Grass, Marty Robbins, Jim Reeves and the rest. It never happened.

It was funny that my years in the RAF had not led me to knock into any Americans that I could talk to, as I toured around such a large part of the world and back—but I can't remember meeting and talking to one, Until, that is, I was back in Scotland, posted to our frozen north, near the town of Peterhead. There, of all places, for the first time, at the age of 22, I actually talked and spent some time with a one hundred per cent American—a lady I met in the local dance hall, and 'dated'. (Before the influence of the talkies, 'dated' was a term not used much in my part of the world; we would 'winch' a pretty girl).

Can you imagine that! After all the moving around and the tidal wave of Americana that had flooded over me—and still kept a comin', this was my first encounter with the American form of the human species; and she was a humdinger too! At the time, Frank Ifield was singing, 'I Remember You'. Huh, he's not the only one who often sings that!

Yet I did hear and see lots of Americans during these years, but, they seemed to be living a separate life; they were the 'aliens', to be observed through a glass-sided box, so to speak. We didn't converse. Why, I don't know. In London, you couldn't visit a pub or restaurant without hearing the loud voice of an American, usually a sailor or soldier. In Scotland, near where I lived, there was an American Air Force base at a place called Kirknewton; and they would descend upon Edinburgh *Palais de Dance* in vast numbers, with lots of money and good looks. I suppose they had been better fed!! Well, they liked a good fight, and they certainly got one.

Picture the massive rectangular dance hall, with an upstairs balcony that ran all around the place. A stramash (punch up) would be going on upstairs, and maybe two more on the dance floor below. This was all happening while the huge revolving bandstand at one end was in the midst of rotating, exchanging one noisy orchestra for another. If I remember right, Sean Connery (or Big Tam, as he was known hereabouts) would occasionally work as a bouncer there.

Sean (Tam) Connery

At that time, he lived literally only yards from the Palais. It could be bedlam, but great fun, with only fists flying. I don't remember anything serious—there seemed no real desire (on either side) to hurt anybody. The fights were usually over a girl, of course; and through Scottish jealousy of the smart American uniforms, the money their rivals could throw around, and how attractive this made them seem.

Meanwhile, in America, even the movie industry wasn't able to escape the hysterical upheaval caused by Joe McCarthy and his anti-communism drive—or rather, charade. Quite a few of the big film stars (and producers) lost their good reputations (even in Britain) because of their perfidious testimonies—sending many good and talented people into la-la land.

Richard Nixon's, with his swarthy looks, fresh from Eisenhower's side, was noteworthy during this evil farce. His cunning intelligence was more than just useful to these sorry persecutors. It was no surprise that he would come to figure large in the later history of the US—in the political field he was 'pressing palms' building bridges, stacking up support for the future—making connections.

While all this was happening, Elvis was blowing everyone away—the whole world rocked, jived and rolled to American rhythms and rhapsodies. Bill Haley and the Comets arrived among us: 'One, two, three o'clock rock'. Tony Bennett sang about little cable cars travelling to the stars and of leaving his heart in San Francisco. Little Richard, Chuck Berry, Roy Orbison, Fats Domino—on and on – the goodies just kept coming.

Amazing performers appeared, like Willie Nelson and Johnny Cash ('the man in black') who would sing in Folsom gaol. We were hit with Woody Guthrie and Pete Seeger songs; with Ginsberg and Kerouac's 'On the road' books—what a fabulous combination of new and exciting wonders tumbled into our hearts and minds in these years—and most issued forth from America.

So, where am I going now with what is starting to look like an Amercan love in? Well, in the celebrated sixties, after the armed services, I saw action as a 'Redcoat' with a famous British holiday organisation; went on to meet the girl I was going to marry, and then to University—much later than was the usual.

It was at this time that the British musical fight-back, so to speak, began: first 'The Beatles', then 'The Stones'. Cliff Richard had paved the way along with 'The Shadows'. A stream of mediocre imitators also surfaced, but, fortunately, there were bands and performers of real talent, such as 'The Who', 'The Searchers', Marty Wilde, Billy Fury et al.

I suppose my memory of the early '60s—of sex, music, sport, is the same as that of everyone else who lived through these years. But I had one or two ingredients of my own: as I said, marriage, university—and finding casual work outside term-time.

Getting into the Edinburgh University faculty that I fancied meant a good pass in another subject. I chose History, and sat down with a 'History of England'—yeah, that's how a history of the UK was (and still is) described.

Infuriating isn't the word to describe the anger and frustration this engenders among Scots, Irish and Welsh in these here British Isles. Imagine someone talking to an American and referring to the USA as Canada or Mexico and you can get near the feeling.

Neither is the monarch Queen of England alone; she is Queen Elizabeth 1, of Scotland and Elizabeth 11 of England!! And when we appropriated our own Stone of Destiny that Edward 1, 'Hammer of the Scots', pinched in the late 1200s, the same English even accused us of stealing. What a cheek, eh!

But where was I? Yep, the other tome I had to study was a History of them there United States of America. I gobbled it all up, from Indian Wars and American Revolution, to the coming of JFK—and I passed the exams with ease. I had already studied the geography of that amazing country, and would go on to learn American History at Honours level (to major in it, in the American language). I was smitten.

The Old Quad - Edinburgh University

While at Uni I met two fascinating Americans, among the hordes who flocked there. One, a fellow mature student was called 'Kinch'. I have forgotten where exactly he came from, but will never forget the memory of him; he was so laid back it made me gasp. That was the first time I had come across this 'hail fellow, well met—and 'let's have a beer' feature of American sociability—and I liked it. He lived and breathed *manyana*.

The other, absolutely awesome, breathtaking American was my lecturer, Dr James (Jim) Compton. He was something else. His lectures, sometimes to two hundred people at a time— they packed in—were a riot of laughter combined with penetrating analyses.

His tutorials that I was privileged to attend (consisting of about ten people) were a revelation. We also learned from him what he considered the perfect tutorial class: around three English people—because, he said, they will talk non-stop, irrespective of whether they know anything at all about the subject in question; at least two Americans, because they shout loudly and sound convincing, though again, they might know very little; an Irishman for his sense of humour; and some Scots, because though they might be able to think, they generally keep quiet until hearing the idiocies coming from the others, and then happily join in with some idiocies of their own.

Jim would play the banjo and guitar; and his farewell party, before heading to one of the California Universities, was transformed into a series of send-off extravaganzas, enjoyed by one and all.

Prof Jim Compton

The Married Man

Now this is where—after such a slow beginning—my new found affair with the United States begins to hot up. Here am I, in my thirties now, lecturing in History, what else, and replete with family, when Margaret, the lady I am married to, brings a new dimension into the whole business.

Apart from her doting on Jim Reeves and Country Music, I discovered that her maternal Grandmother, and Grandfather (a blacksmith and farrier) had moved from North-East Scotland to Cody, Wyoming, in 1911, leaving a daughter (Margaret's mother) and another child behind in Scotland, to be looked after 'by the folks back home'. From Cody, Margaret's grandparents moved to Sheridan, where they had more children to add to the ones who had been left behind.

Their descendants are still there and also in greater Chicago and spread all over Illinois. We even had a visit from a cousin from the Chicago area.

The family in Scotland blame Buffalo Bill's visit to Scotland for this exodus. They think that William Cody's wonderful circus of Indians, horses, rodeos, and such, hypnotised the blacksmith-cum-farrier so much, he just had to get 'to the land of the free'.

The Presidency of John Fitzgerald Kennedy (despite all we now know about his private life) was accurately defined then (and now) as heralding a new and better time. The Irish, in particular, but most people I spoke to over here, enthused about 'Camelot'.

We did not like the support for South American dictators, however; nor the Republican—Democrat stand-offs; nor the Cuban business, and the Bay of Pigs; and were scared 'as all hell' (another Americanism) by the confrontation with Kruschev over missiles in Cuba.

And here I go again on this subject, nor did we like the growth of what seemed to us as rather sinister organisations (the CIA, FBI) and the spying that went on. 'Hoover' became a dirty word (laugh - please!).

The 'Mob', as you call organised crime, the mixing of Hollywood glamour with politics and the Mafia, were greeted with unconcealed disbelief here. We had plenty of crooks—but even Britain's 'Great Train Robbery' of those years was never on this scale.

◆◆◆

Meanwhile, 'back at the ranch', so to speak, the excitement issuing from across 'the pond' continued to affect us mere mortals. American home and foreign affairs were generating a tremendous amount of conversation. Hollywood led, as usual: Marlon Brando, Doris Day, James Dean, Marilyn Munro, Liz Taylor and Burton; the activities of the 'Rat Pack' in Las Vegas; the list is endless and I could be naming them from 'here to eternity'.

The incomparable Marilyn Munro

We had already fallen in love with 'Flower Power' and left our hearts in San Francisco, succumbing to Cass Elliot and that fellow, Scott Mackenzie.
Also, the space race was on; the Russians had sent a dog into the Cosmos; and now a man, Yuri Gagarin.

'We will send a man to the Moon', said President Kennedy, in response, and before the 1960s had ended so they had. But neither John F Kennedy, nor his father, Old Joe, nor his brother, Robert, would be there to see it.

President John F Kennedy

1960s - Memories
The Kennedy assassination is still, by far, the blackest moment in America's recent, if not whole history, outwith the events of the Civil War. The motives and mystery underlying Lincoln's death we see clearly, as also that of the two other Presidents murdered: Garfield and McKinley, not to mention the twenty or so other attempts to do away with other Leaders of the Nation.

What is so galling, even to an 'alien', is that the Warren Report giving the official description of the Jack Kennedy shooting, stating that only one gunman was involved, is so obviously wrong it is beneath comment.

The Zapruder film, covering the whole 'Grassy Knoll' incident, clearly shows a bullet striking the President in the front of his head, making it jerk back, and was never, as alleged, a reaction to the bullet entering the back of the head.

Here we are, 50 years on, and we can see Jackie Kennedy reaching back over the rear of the car, in a futile attempt, as her bodyguard confirms, to try and rescue parts of her husband's hair, skin and scalp that had been blown backwards by the striking bullet.

It has now been discovered that parts of the President's brain have mysteriously disappeared from where they were kept!!

The alleged conspiracies are endless; and Lee Oswald, together with his killer, Jack Ruby remain unresolved puzzles within this ongoing mystery.

The Fatal Motorcade in Dallas

These macabre statistics illustrate the 'American Nightmare' that rides alongside the 'American Dream'; and the American people are not alone in wondering what was going on at this terrible time—even more so with the whole stream of dreadful events that followed.

There was ongoing, incredible anger at the treatment of blacks (anger not confined to America): the segregation in buildings, in buses, in schools, to name only a few of a stream of indignities.

Civil Rights saw the march on Birmingham, Alabama; Martin Luther King's 'I have a dream' speech, from the steps of the Lincoln memorial.

The killing of this man and the murder of Robert Kennedy—all in so short a space of time—was stupefying.

Dr Martin Luther King Junior "I have a dream"

What had happened? The world still does not know; but such has been the impact of a tidal wave of America's culture, via all means of communication for such a long time, it has deeply and equally affected all non-Americans. Such awareness of America's recent history from the point of its entry into the 2nd World War, at least; and the way that it has dwarfed all other nations in just about every field, means the world wants to know.

♦♦♦

The major thing to strike me regarding all this is that beforehand, I had rejoiced at America's apparent open-ness, something I had found refreshing when compared to the layer upon layer of British bureaucracy that leaves the individual with nobody to get a grip of, no one to approach or speak to regarding a problem. The feeling here, with regard to British officialdom, has always been one of sinking into a swamp, one that slowly encloses questioner and question until all is lost or forgotten.

Yet, even Oliver Stone has not been able to get to the root—or at least find the proof—of what was going on in the US then. Perhaps it is still going on today. Many recent films highlighting semi-secret American agencies appear to suggest as much: The 'Bourne Identity' for instance, appears to touch upon a fear of such developments—all in the pursuit of defence and patriotism, of course.

Vietnam, I don't have to remind anyone, was a sickening business. The many civilian deaths; young men killed, for what? The horrifying pictures of a man being assassinated, a bullet in the head, right in front of the camera; of young, naked children burned beyond hope by napalm.

The authotities 'back home' faced a nightmare. There was wringing of hands by those who had to face the Communist connundrum in the east; likewise daily confrontation with the violent, but easily understood opposition on the campuses. There was naked anguish at having to deal with those who wanted to avoid the draft; of facing up to the brutalization and despair of the troops. What to do, what to do. Presidents and advisors, alike, had no answer. The general American public did not believe in the 'Domino' theory, that the east would turn red. They wanted the boys returned home.

From Academic (Ph.D. and College Lecturer) to Businessman

From what you have read so far—starting with Hollywood films and even my conversations, latterly, with real Americans—it is clear some sort of association with America had been going on all my life, long-distance, so to speak.

From 1984, however, this long-distance arrangement would change. I became an hotelier, in Edinburgh; and such is the allure of this magnificent city, crowned by its Castle on a rock (Wimpey didn't build it) I now began to meet and speak to many. Edinburgh, with a spectacular setting of mountains, sea and sky, is inundated with American tourists.

The hotel experience, on the whole, was a good one—if you like people and they like you. Fortunately, both descriptions fitted my wife and I. We were hoteliers until 1999.

Most American visitors were courteous, interested and had a streak of laughter in them. Obviously, we had the exceptions, and as usual they are the ones you remember: those who were expecting a 5 star hotel, while paying ordinary bed and breakfast rates; the psychotic, psychologist, who wanted my kids to take her to their school, where she would show the teacher how to teach. We gave her three beds to choose from: hard, medium and soft. She slept on the floor—or so she said.

A wonderful US Attorney and his wife, who hailed from San Franciso kept comparing Edinburgh, The Forth Rail Bridge, our hills and scenery, to his city. I told him, 'We have a better bridge than the 'Golden Gate. So there!!' He agreed.

The Assistant DA, from Phoenix, entertained with his hairy stories of the hoodlums he had met. You should have seen my kids' eyes go pop!

The Doctor from Los Angeles, when we asked about his city, could only mutter 'L.A. is a Zoo'.

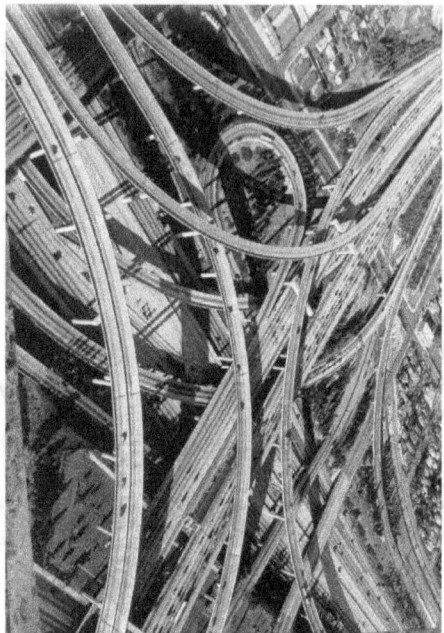

Just a little road junction in LA

A man and wife from Seattle we only found out later were incredibly rich, because he left his digital camera behind. This showed power boats, massive houses and lawns. In the note of thanks for sending the camera to them, they said they had just wanted to stay with an ordinary Scottish family. Are we ordinary? I dunno!!

Earlier in this tourism and catering business, we were rather forced to 'look after' a New York guy, Jeff Silver. He had run out of money, and, we found out, had also run away from Manhattan. His was only one of many similar cases—but at least he didn't 'do a runner'; he was honest and above board about everything. I often wonder what became of him.

The most wonderful thing of all, I have to say, was the genuine friendships we made, with fellow-Britons, with Australians, Canadians, Europeans, Egyptians and, for sure, Americans.

Before going on to tell you about our hook-up with the Virginians, who became our friends, let me say a bit about one or two of the others. Bill and Helen Marshall, from the Gold Coast, just south of Brisbane, Australia, would hurry back to us, after touring the Highlands, the lochs and glens. They always talked about returning to their 'home' in Scotland, i.e. us. Needless to say, they visited on more than one occasion, and Bill and I were able to share once more our love of golf.

'The Holy of Holies' St Andrews

Hotelier Experience...,continued..

In Edinburgh, at breakfast, one morning, we had the comical sight of two mature Americans in pursuit of our milk man on his pony and cart, who had just delivered the daily supply. The reason for this? Well, we just happened to mention it was the same horse and cart used by Sean Connery when he delivered the milk!

'Big Tam's' Edinburgh St Cuthbert's Milk Cart?

Later, we moved on to own another hotel, but two Canadian sisters, with their husbands in tow, tracked us down for yet another visit. We also had the old French gentleman, whose snores could be heard issuing from his open window a mile up the street. No; he didn't snort with a French accent!

Then there was the great figure of our stand-out Egyptian guest. I discovered he liked a taste of 'the cratur' (whisky) and he would sit in the dining room at breakfast time (believe it or not) sipping away peacefully. Our very own Pharaoh was a great hunched figure, all jowls and heavily-lidded eyes. The other visitors tried not to look as they breakfasted, but failed dismally. I still don't know if he was Muslim.

Even when the sign said "Full-up", he wouldn't go away. On one occasion we fixed him up elsewhere with overnight accommodation—but he was back with his tooth brush at 9am next morning.

He owned or was director of an Egyptian newspaper, and the night before leaving asked if we would arrange a call through to his Cairo office regarding travel arrangements. This we duly did, informing the operator at our end to make sure the Egyptians at the other end "Arranged for Hannay Camel to collect him from the airport".

Friendship with our Virginian family continues to this day. It now incorporates all our family members, and many wonderful neighbours of theirs.

One of these amazing people, in her 90s, stems from the Doswell family of Virginia, famous as great horse breeders. In the 1700s, their horse, 'Planet', a 'Great Red', was the first 'cuddy' (horse in our language) to win every leading track event of the day.

There is also a connection with 'Secretariat', the other 'Great Red', which in more recent times has also won every top race in the US; and has even had a movie made about him.

Ashland Virginia

The European and World Cultural Fight Back

Around this time in my life, if I have managed to recollect everything in their proper sequence, my attitude to things European—which until then was positively secondary to American culture—shifted somewhat. This was certainly the case as far as literature, music and art were concerned. 'Gargantua' and 'Pantagruel', from the pen of Rabelais were now more than appreciated; Dumas, Heine and Goethe as well, together with countless other authors from all over the Continent. In music, it was the same, a recognition of what I had been missing: Mascagni's Intermezzo from 'Cavalleria Rusticana'; Puccini, Tschaikovsky, Mendelsshohn, Brahms, Schubert, Chopin and Mozart—the list of geniuses goes on and on.

Singers—such as Caruso, Jussi Bjorling (especially with Robert Merrill in 'The Pearl Fishers'), Melba, Callas, Tebaldi, Netrebko, Te Kanewa, Pavarotti, Placido Domingo—and even Richard Tauber—were now a part of my life.

Visits to art galleries made me more than aware of European treasures and of other wonders from the world at large. I now appreciated the skill, the genius and intelligence stored for posterity in the form of sculptures: such as those of Rodin or the statue of 'David' by Michaelangelo; the matchless canvases of Van Dyke, Renoir, Monet and Manet; the Dutch masters: Van Gogh, the Vermeers, Breughel the Elder, Bosch, Hals, and above all, Rembrandt.

In Amsterdam I had the pleasure of seeing just about every painting by this master in an exhibition at the Rijksmuseum located in the Dam square; an experience rounded off by an insightful anaysis by an expert of 'The Night Watch'.

♦♦♦

American Travelogue

In 1991, I made my first foray into the States, accompanied by my wife, Margaret. She was needed to keep me on the straight and narrow with so much to see and do. [From now on, forgive me if I switch between 'I', 'we', 'me', 'us' in the narrative. My better half has been with me on all my travels and it gets a bit of a habit to refer to what *we* both saw and did.] This first visit was followed by others: in 2002, 2003, 2005 and 2011. Hopefully, many more will transpire.

So, there was I, in the spring of that year, face to face for the first time, with a world that had always facinated me. Heck, during my RAF days I was almost drafted to Washington DC, but just missed out; later I had contemplated enrolling as a student there. My wife tells me that she heard this from me, maybe just two days after we first met. 'Nuff said.

So what was my impression of America from these visits? I'll give the verdict first and then tell you about the places and folk we ran into.

Ordinary American people—and I mean nearly all—are probably the most courteous I have met in all my travels. They are friendly, good mannered and—on the surface at least—interested in you. However, 'Have a good day', though meant well, becomes rather wearisome. In a first visit to America the sheer space and dimensions are mindblowing, certainly for people from a small, crowded island like Britain (though we Scots do have the last European wilderness, so they say). But even after subsequent trips, the countryside seems just endless, going on for mile after mile, after mile. It does make me envious.

I also thoroughly approve of the care taken by so many to maintain America's beauty; and I can only applaud the impression left with me overall, that no matter how humble someone's abode, an effort is made to make it look good. Having said that, I know you have the same 'couldn't care less' individuals that we do—characters who have no pride. The same limitless space has also led to carelessness: There seems to be no legislation governing the setting up of signs alongside the road; the dumps, huge brown earth lots and wastelands, both in cities and open countryside, these are appearing more monotonously. What about all those old aeroplanes just lying about in acres and acres of desert? Progress? Bah!

The motels in America are first-class, well, most of them, anyway. (I'm going to forget that bad experience in Orlando, the one with the water-bed!!) Talking about beds, they are so big! Now I dearly love the king sized ones.

Then there are the road networks, which are very good indeed, especially the Inter-States. That said, there's perhaps a sameness about the rest-up places and eating joints: KFC, MacDonalds and the like. And why are the meals so huge? And what about the loud American voices you hear.

Nevertheless, one of my most beloved, and abiding memories, is a vocal one: "Where y'all from?"—which issues from the lips of nearly everyone you meet—especially when in the southern states. Another never to be forgotten sound came from the lips of a huge black conductor. As the Amtrak train approached the Capital he made his way down the passageway, shouting at the top of his voice, "Next stop Waaa—aaashington". It was a great moment, and stuck a grin on everyone's face.

What have I not liked or missed?

No castles, palaces, old stone buildings. When I say old, I mean medieval. No ruins, no monastries and the like. So many timber houses, usually of a clapboard design.
The sameness of the food: on the whole it's bland—especially the cheese.
Eating on the run—where did that come from? It's not good for the digestion.
When in restaurants, hearing every conversation within a radius of ten yards, like it or lump it. Calculated tips based on cost of food eaten, I am not sure about that development.
Lack of knowledge, and in many cases, lack of interest, outwith the area in which the people you are talking to live.

I am now quite used to driving on the right—having had to contend with Europe as well; also staying in lane; and I keep a wary eye on the studs of the big trucks plowing up and down the Inter-States. They come tearing up behind you—at eye level this is a monstrous sight, especially when you are driving a Mustang; and they 'aint goin' to stop' for you or anyone!!

What about the wonders I have seen there? Have they lived up to my dreams?
Of course they have: Seeing the coast of the North American continent for the first time, as the plane followed the Great Circle route: New Foundland giving way to the St Lawrence, to the New England coastline. It still lives in my mind.

Ashland, Virginia: the railtrack running through the centre of the town en-route to Richmond and the south. Hearing the 'Orange Blossom Special' as she proceeded northwards, replete with hundreds of tanks full of 'kindness and vitality' from Florida. The train took around fifteen minutes to pass through, until at last the haunting note of the whistle (one I had heard in countless screen Westerns) retreated in the distance. Realising this was the same track along which most of the Civil War had been fought.

Visiting sites: redoubts, the same ones occupied by soldiers from the north and the south at various stages in the fighting. Gardens full of old stirrups, gold buttons, bullets; examining private collections. Tracing a portion of Robert E. Lee's military movements; and scrutinizing the museum made over to him; visiting Appomatox and the realization of what it meant: that the Union would survive.

Other Exquisite Places on our first visit:

The journey to Richmond, on to Jamestown and crossing the broad James River; to Yorktown and Williamsburg; wallowing in the history of the birth of the nation that these journeys brought to mind.

The expedition to Monticello, to pay our respects to Jefferson—and the thought that the Scottish Enlightenment was central to the views of this man and his fellows, those who had drawn up the Constitution. Also, that so many Scots had become Presidents and provided leadership in other fields, such as Witherspoon's contribution to Princeton.

Monticello - Jefferson's 'Litle Bittie Home'

I will never forget our journey along the Blue Ridge trail, singing Laurel and Hardy's 'Lone Pine Tree' song; or the short trip to 'The Neck', a portion of land projecting out into the Chesapeake, where the old Scots traders bought the tobacco for sale and built warehouses for the crop—so long ago.

I also believe what I was told by Virginians: that Stephen Foster's song, 'The Camptown ladies sing this song, Doo-da, Doo-da' originated not far from Ashland; that 'The Camptown racetrack five miles long, Oh, de doo-da day', was situated there. So, for a couple of days, I was singing: 'Goin' to run all night/ Goin' to run all day/I bet my money on a bob-tailed nag/ somebody bet on the grey.'

Then to Washington! What can I say? It was very, very special. We had seen the whole central portion of the city from the sky when flying in: the Capitol, the Lincoln memorial, the central plaza and waterway, the Washington monument; the Supreme Court, the Jefferson Temple and other beautiful, white buildings.

I think what surprised me most, however, was the number of joggers—they were everywhere, and I believe a President or two could be found among them, showing off some skinny knees.

Without doubt, the most emotional visit was to Arlington: Rank after rank of white crosses, over dale, down through glades, mile after mile of well-tended graves: the never-to-be-forgotten dead from America's wars.

They made me think of De Toqueville's remark, dating from the eighteenth century, that America's power would be unbelievable if and when she applied herself to arms; but, it also seemed to me, as I looked upon this never-ending tragedy, at what a cost!

Naturally JFK's eternal flame—and Bobby's grave alongside—created tremendous emotional turmoil inside me; as did coming to Audi Murphy's plot and seeing two old ladies plant Cherry blossom beside the two little American flags on his grave.

It was a similar feeling when visiting the Korean War Memorial and the 'The Wall' that commemorates those who fell in the Vietnam War whose names are inscribed there.

I think there were really only two things we disliked: In Arlington, American marines provided an eerie spectacle: marching with rifles in a fashion that allowed no natural bobbing up and down movement: heads remained fixed in one place in space and time, and each platoon glided along the paved floor of the Remembrance Auditorium. This manner of movement by such a formidable body of men was so eerily quiet and deadly, so full of intent, it made me shudder.

The other disconcerting feature that sticks in the mind, were groups of black men in the city, gathered at corners, their liquor in brown paper pokes. (Only in America have we found this done).

They were not threatening, rather the opposite, forlorn. (A similar picture would emerge in San Franciso, on a later trip: of black men rolled up in newspapers, sleeping in the doorways lining the public thoroughfare.)

More Features from the 1991 and 2003 Visits

In the course of our first vacation in 1991 and again in 2003 (I will deal with 2002 later) we journeyed further into the Deep South, to Florida.

The first expedition (1991) went: Boston, Detroit, Washington, Tampa; the second (2003): Washington, Boston, Tampa; and both return trips were via Dulles airport, Washington.

Air travel was like being on a bus back home in Scotland: people were queuing to get off almost before the plane landed.

Boston was cold on the second visit; the 'Big Dig' was in progress; and although most of the sights were taken in (even had a drink in 'Cheers' bar) we seemed to go everywhere walking under glass cover because it was so chilly.

St Pete's Florida

36

In Florida, St. Pete's and Clearwater elicited admiration; as did the pelicans, the very impressive Skyway Bridge over Tampa Bay—on our way to Saratoga, and playing golf—what a clubhouse! However, I think it strikes most visitors, right away, that Florida's marvellous climate and out of this world tourist atractions, make it quite different from other states.

All of the Orlando attractions are certainly a must for a first visit: Disney World, Epcot, the film studios; but for me, not places to go back to, apart, perhaps, for Seaworld.

Kissimmee, with its beautiful houses, gave a feel of the luxury and ostentation that a great many Americans enjoy—but the number of gated communities also gave a glimpse of the security needed.

A visit to the Kennedy Space station to view NASA's achievements, followed by a run down the east coast towards Miami was a journey I wish everyone could make. Cocoa beach—we love you.

By this time, I was well-used to the massive shopping malls, overhead traffic signals; storms and lightning appearing from nowhere—I am told I am lucky to be alive, just missing one earth-bound strike in the St Pete's region.

The Everglades, the birds, snakes, reptiles— especially 'gators lying in the bunkers on the golf courses; the heat and the 'vital' air-conditioners—all this has to be experienced.

It was also awesome being held in awe by some people because I had played St Andrews golf course, Muirfield, Gleneagles, Turnberry, and so on.

(Why does everyone say 'awesome' and 'Oh My God' over there—and now here?) As far as golf is concerned, in the good old USA it is all so...so...democratic...but only if you have the money. Not so in Scotland, though we too have our bastins of privilege!!

◆◆◆

2002 — Music Tour of some Southern States

Now, let me tell you about the 2002 tour, which really did let me meet the ordinary American 'Joe', because, after flying into New Orleans from Washington, most of the rest of the journey was by hired car—and what a journey it turned out to be.

First, New Orleans itself. (Remember, this was before 'Katrina', the storm that almost destroyed the city). Quite simply, it was amazing: Bourbon Street and the jazz (inside and out on the streets); Cajun music played out on the road by various groups—some artistes wearing Stetsons, and growing long fluffy beards.

After nightfall, ladies on balconies were desperate to allow the passing throng a glimpse of what nature had endowed them with. Streamers and banners; eating grits for the first time, it was all magical. Sailing up the Mississippi on a great big Showboat, 'The Creole Queen' with its (imitation) paddles thrashing, while eating crayfish and listening to a great jazz band. Setting out from Canal Street, seated in an original old tram to visit the leafy and green suburb of Garden City. What an atmosphere - more magic! Then next day, we were off on the next stage of this great adventure.

37

Bourbon Street, New Orleans

The first remarkable, thing leaving New Orleans, was the feeling of skimming about two inches above water—well, we were, above Lake Ponchertrain. (When later, Katrina struck, and the dykes were broken—we remembered how near water we were at all times—with the mighty Mississippi always there).

Mile after mile, as we travelled north through the state with the same name, we were aware of that mighty flow of water just a little to the west of us, with only the occasional crossing via very peculiar looking girder bridges.

Natchez, Vicksburg, Civil War sites; riverboats used as floating casinos—on through the Delta—heading towards Clarksville and a reconnoitre, we hoped, with people in that birthland of blues music who had known the great names, like Muddy Waters and John Lee Hooker. Unfortunately, it did not happen.

A wonderful moment, en-route, however, was the stop at a wayside eating place. As we entered, a gorgeous, huge black lady looked up at me, opened her arms and announced: 'He's mine'.

My wife got a lovely smile. We were then treated to the largest and best steak rolls that I think I have ever tasted, juices just running out of them.

Memphis, Tennessee

Our next stop was Memphis. The hotel overlooked the ball park and a game was going on; there were huge crowds.

Next day, Beale Street, Bebe King and the Blues; Sun Recording studios; Schwab's store (which had just about everything in it—including a faded photo of Elvis when living in Tupelo); a bus tour around the city; then next day, Graceland and Elvis. I was struck very deeply by the evidence of the star's never ending gifts to charity. This side of him seldom gets aired. When friends, back home, are told of paying our tribute to the King, the envy seeps out of them. Rightly or wrongly, he is still loved and admired by a great many.

Elvis

The jealousy back home becames worse when we tell of Jackson, Tennessee, our next stop. We stayed the night beside Casey Jones and the 'Runaway train' that 'came over the hill and she blew'—still parked off main street. These good friends are then sunk out of sight with the tale of our run across Tennessee. (I like the sound of that word—good to say slowly, Ten-e-see) that took in Nashville, visits to Grand Old Opry and all the rest, simply to hear first hand, almost to feel, 'that there Country Music'.

The plantation that had belonged to President Andrew Jackson, 'Old Hickory' drew us next. From the farming set up examined, what was made very plain to us was the different kind of life led by the rich of those days—a world removed from that inhabited by their slaves (and those enjoying supposed freedom after 1865), as well as that of poor white people.

From there, we headed south to see 'Ruby Falls', a waterfall deep in the heart of a mountain on the north side of Chattanooga. We found the cascade in a cave, hiding beneath millions of tons of earth and rock; and everything was bathed in a sort of wine-coloured light, with soft music playing. Unbelievable!

The guide held an impromptu check on where we all came from. Needless to say, we were the only ones from Scotland, a fact that elicited quite a few gasps of amazement—especially from a party of Chicagoans (Is that the right term?)

They were not to know that near this area (and also incorporating territory in Alabama and Georgia) travelled an eighteenth century ancestor from Scotland, Lachlan McGillivary, who started out as a trader.

He married a Cree Indian Princess, and went on to build trading-posts among the Upper Towns of the Muscogee Confederacy. In 1783, his son, Alexander McGillivray became the principal chief of the Upper Creek towns.

He was also largely responsible for squeezing $6 million out of George Washington as recompense to the Cree for land dealings. He is to be congratulated—it was hard to get anything out of dear old George in 'them thar days'.

From Chattanooga, we struck east, then south, across the Smoky Mountains, going via Knoxville, Pigeon Forge, Gatlinburg, Cherokee and Maggie Valley. The stop-over in Pigeon Forge led to an unexpected Country and Western show in Dolly Parton's entertainment complex. All the male guitarists wore big stetson hats—it seemed to be *de rigueur*, making half of their heads disappear from sight! I don't think it was meant to be funny—it was hilarious.

The show that night also led to an insight into the mind-set of mid-America.
'Where y'all from?' asked my neighbour in the next seat. His wife was on his left flank, my wife on my right.
'From Edinburgh, Scotland', said I. There was a disconcerted look on his face. I knew he didn't have a clue where that was, and he leaned over to enquire of his wife. She didn't know either. To save embarrassment I asked about him, where was he from?
'Oh, I have a small spread over there (he meant over the Mississippi); run a couple of thousand head of cattle'.
'That must be miles away', I said. He agreed, in fact it was more than a hundred of them. He then went on to say that folks, thereabouts, thought nothing of a four hundred miles round trip. In a round about fashion his good wife again asked where we were from. We answered, across the Atlantic, which we guessed they had heard of, and left it at that.

Next, it was on to sighting black bears as we climbed upwards over Gatlinburg in a cable car; and to our question, put to some puzzled Americans, 'What's an RV?', we received some withering looks. Stupid us, we didn't know anything about the 'recreational vehicles' they had been talking about!

And why was there a fireworks factory in Cherokee? No answer. We seemed to find these factories all over the States. Nuthin' like that our side of the pond.

Spartanburg, North Carolina, came and went; it gave way to Eureka, Lancaster, Florence, Conway and onwards to Myrtle Beach, where we thought we would rest up for a couple of days beside the sea.

This part of America, just passed through, gave the impression of being very fertile, with prosperous looking towns and people; altogether, a very fine area to live in. Myrtle Beach was a beautiful place—and to my delight overflowing with golf courses and golf shops.

Myrtle Beach

In the ritzy hotel we stopped at, the receptionist left me open-mouthed when she asked if I knew anything about Admiral Lord Cochrane, a Scot famous for a whole list of achievements. Foremost among these was winning sea battles (used by Patrick O'Brien for 'Master and Commander', and brought to life in the film starring Russell Crowe). Cochrane also formed navies for the likes of Chile and Greece, as well as upsetting the high and mighty Lords of the British Admiralty. As you can imagine, I liked him. Well, this girl was married to a direct descendant of the man; and she was bowled over when I quoted chapter and verse on her fella's great, great, great grandpappy; and I couldn't get over meeting someone like her in Myrtle Beach.

We had set our sights on reaching Savannah, using all the back-roads and missing out Charleston on the way south. En-route we held a never-ending discussion regarding which part of the coastline 'Blackbeard' the pirate might have beached his ship upon—perhaps there's gold in 'them thar sand dunes.'

Blackbeard

I also think that drive let us experience more of the 'heartland' than any other. Even outside the most tumble-down shack 'Old Glory' fluttered. Every few miles there was a church of some sort. A station waggon stood outside or alongside most doors. There was little evidence of much money among these poor people, yet a feeling of relaxation and happiness.

Savannah was everything we expected: the lovely old squares; learning of the important Scottish presence there in the early eighteenth century; seeing the public building with its golden top; and Forrest Gump's famous bench. Asian Indians with the name 'Patel' were everywhere (the equivalent of 'Smith'). Most of all, the memory of sipping a great big 'Bloody Mary' in a restaurant on the river waterfront, while a mere six feet away, a massive cargo ship silently glided by on her way downriver. It was like a whole tenement slipping past your eyes.

Tybee was next. What a beach! What wide open skies! A baptism was going on at a spot on the beach below the jetty we watched from. The restaurants had fabulous fish dishes; and we were getting used to seeing Americans at breakfast time making their own pancakes using a funny looking machine, then smothering them with maple syrup (the pancakes, I mean). Such sweetness—and first thing in the morning!! On the way back to Savannah we spotted the house of Johnny Mercer, the great song writer. He could conjure up a fine ditty.

Another memory of Tybee (apart from its splendour) centres on the job we had finding spirits to drink. Beer could be had in plenty, from every store, but alcohol in any other form— believe me, that was a different matter. After finding the liquor shop—way at the end of the town—we asked the lady why this was so. She had no answer and agreed it was a real give away to be seen with a package covered in brown paper!

By mistake, I took the road to Atlanta—well, let's face it, 'The Masters' was going on. I like my golf and the old sub-conscious must have been at work. Correcting the gaffe and finally getting onto the correct road via an exciting detour, we next visited a typical plantation. This was approached through an avenue of trees, all of which were swathed in purple-coloured 'Spanish Moss'. It was beautiful.

We finally reached Charleston; yet another terrific hotel at ordinary prices. A visit to Sullivan Island was followed by views of Fort Sumpter and of the massive aircraft carrier—just parked alongside the road!! Then, once a peculiar set of road bridges were negotiated, we found ourselves in the regal setting of mid-town.

Aircraft Carrier at Charleston

That is where we learned about the fruits and flowers represented on each vehicle's number plate; and saw Jack Vetriano's paintings for sale in the local shops. 'The Singing Butler' was given great prominence.

To put you in the picture, the work of this man, from Fife, Scotland, sells by the ton, but the hoi-poloi of the British art world will not place his work in the galleries. They are mad; the ordinary man in Scotland is not daft, however, and neither are Americans.

The Singing Butler

From there, it was a short aeroplane hop to Washington, then another to Richmond and our friends in Ashland.

The flight to the capital of Virginia was memorable for the sight of the one and only steward, a great big black lad, easily six feet four inches and wide with it, trying to negotiate his way along the narrow passage between the rows of seats. He sweated some, but he didn't give up and we all received our jollies!

The journey later, from Ashland up to Dulles Airport by car, will be remembered always, because our Virginians had a pamphlet that told you of civil war sites we would come across on that particular route.

As we approached the little road signs indicating where an important engagement had taken place we were able to read of it from this book and tick it off.

For some reason the one for 'Second Bull Run' (or Manassas) in Prince William County, sticks in my memory.

2005—the West

As I said earlier, together with friends we visited again, in 2003: Boston, Tampa and Kissimmee. Then, in 2005, we were in the USA once more.

In between times, the American connnection was kept alive through visits from The Virginians. (Does anyone remember the TV series with that title?) They were accompanied by other friends of theirs from Virgina and North Carolina.

This time, however, we were on our way to the Golden State, to San Francisco. From there we had arranged to fly to Las Vegas, then to Los Angeles. And once more words can scarce describe the places and the people we met, all so different.

Looking back, San Francisco probably made the biggest impression as a place you might like to live in. Yes, we reached towards the sun in a little (crowded) cable car; visited Fisherman's Wharf; saw the sea lions sprawled in the sun; looked out to Alcatraz—which we then sailed past in a tourist boat.

We saw many of the places mentioned during the sixties, the time of free love and the flower people; passed through Ashbury Heights; looked across to the bridge that spanned Oakland Bay; took photographs at the Golden Gate Bridge and visited the park beside it.

The gardens had been designed by a Scot—they get everywhere. We liked Union Square; the shopping, which seemed to suit most people, price wise; and even visited a pub called 'Edinburgh Castle'.

Union Square, San Francisco

44

Then it was off to the casino Mecca of the world: Las Vegas, Nevada. The flight over the Sierra was fabulous; the descent into the sand basin, with the city at its centre, already gleaming with light from the famous strip, unbelievable.

One-armed slot machines come to meet passengers as they step off the plane. These 'money-takers' were never far away until stepping on board again, three days later. Visits to the famous places followed, such as Caesars Palace. Food was excellent; the variety shows wonderful value. I'm sure Elvis would have been amazed at the numbers and the variety of his imitators; but he remains, simply the best.

The heat was impossible to bear, it clutched at the throat; sweat stains could be felt spreading inexorably over most parts of the body. Watching people stick their credit cards into a machine, then sit and gamble away all their money broke my heart. I think we risked $10. Not our scene at all.

The visit to the Grand Canyon was a different matter: Lake Mead, the Hoover Dam, Boulder City en-route; the Joshua trees, and finally, Eagle Point and fabulous views of the Colorado far, far below, a strip of blue, lined with green. The eagle shaped formation of the rocks opposite was, indeed, truly magnificent. The local Indian tribe, the Hualapai, owning the entire tourist rights, were there to meet each visiting bus: meals, trinkets, photograph sessions. (Today, there is a viewing platform, semi-circular in shape that juts way out over the edge, providing a terrifying view around and below, through the glass walkway).

The Grand Canyon at Eagle Point

45

Then it was Los Angeles, LAX airport. The city is just massive (and the airport too). The taxi travelled miles to our abode, the old Queen Mary. The liner was berthed at Long Beach alongside a Russian submarine dating from the days of the Soviet Union.

Though aged and a little worn in places, what a fabulous setting this unique ship provided: state cabins gave way to superb dining facilities and to ward rooms where we might sample the 'barley bree' (whisky)—especially in the bar located on the Bridge.

We could wander all over the ship, see the Captain's Quarter-Deck, visit engines, crawl and climb everywhere we desired. She was (I just have to say it) built by John Brown, on the River Clyde, in Scotland.

Each day, we went somewhere different: locally, a visit to a genuine 1950s-1960s soda fountain cafe; meals in restaurants with magnificent settings—many looking out towards the gigantic liner.

Then, it seems, we did something that made quite a few people shiver when they heard: we travelled to mid-Los Angeles using the local train network—through areas not deemed too safe or respectable. Yet, apart from seeing one old lady who seemed to be carrying all her belongings under the woolen hat she wore, and two young cyclists, who let off a stink bomb before departing the train, it all went fine.

Central LA led us to Hollywood, naturally, and we saw all the sights: Hollywood Boulevard, Sunset Strip, the Chinese Theatre, the star-studded pavement; and simply goggled at where the stars had slept or lived.

Typical rubbernecks, you will say, and would be right. A visit to Venice beach can only be described as weird and wonderful. On view was every kind of body apparel there (nearly) is; and every kind of human behaviour.

I wouldn't have missed it for anything.

Hollywood

♦ ♦ ♦

After that came the *piece de resistance*: we joined the *Monarch of the Seas*, for a four day trip that would take in San Diego, Catalina Island, and Ensenada, Mexico.

The ship was magnificent; it had everything on board that could be desired: from swimming pools, bars, casinos, cinemas, theatres, shops, walls for climbers to hang by their finger tips, lounges, and so many dining rooms it was possible to graze like a goat all day long. Our cabin was what we call 'the bees' knees'—it was excellent.

It got even better. The table we were placed at for the main evening meal—an event in itself—consisted of as varied a collection of idiosyncratic individuals as it was possible to have. We got on like a house on fire. Naturally, not being American made my wife and I the centre of attention—helped by Margaret celebrating a birthday (I'll not say which one).

The lady from Hawaii, who sold real estate, had her daughter (from LA) for company. They were great fun, and aimed at buying silver when at Ensenada. From them, we were blessed with the secret of where to find the best Margarittas in town—and this proved true. We found ourselves seated in a real vaquero type saloon, replete with guitars, people who could strum the instruments, and genuine locals.

The others at the table on board ship included a lad with Mexican ancestry and his pretty new wife; two fabulous ladies (we think they were mothers and married) who had run away from Phoenix on the spur of the moment, 'Just for the hell of it' as one of them put it.

The chap from Rochester, New York state was something else. He and his wife arrived at our table on the second day out, pleading to be allowed to join. 'All we want is someone who will talk to us', said he.

The following morning we were in San Diego, tied up in front of the town, alongside sailing ships modelled on those used in films from 'Treasure Island' to 'Pirates of the Caribbean'. Imitation trees decorated with shoes were strung right along the waterfront. What was that all about?

The Shoe Tree

The start of the 'Santa Fe' railtrack was unmissable, with a locomotive and carriages standing at the platform that just seemed to beckon us to climb aboard. It would have been good to have done so, and heard the last 'All aboard' from the attendant.

The sky scrapers rose before us, trailing up the hill. The city seemed to be filled with little squares, the buildings brightly painted in all colours. Bicycle rickshaws abounded.

I imagined meeting and speaking with Raymond Chandler, who lived hereabouts for some years. We would meet, I dreamed, in a city bar, and I would be discussing with him the writing techniques employed in 'The Big Sleep' and his other books. Fat chance—eh?

Seated on a little tourist train we jogged around the bay to the Zoo; past the hotel where they filmed the fabulous, 'Some Like it Hot', starring Mailyn Munro, Jack Lemmon, Tony Curtis, Joe E Brown and George Raft.

This hotel, right by the sea, looked even better in colour than in the black and white film.Then we heard of a bloke paying $1 million for an apartment looking out to sea—only to have a building erected slap in front of his pad six months later.

Another interesting feature: half the US Navy's high-brass seems to have retired to here!

Avalon, Catalina Island

We sailed on, to Catalina, which was beautiful, with a visit to the tiny airfield at the top of a hill. Looking down at the massive ship in the Avalon bay as the bus was descending, was a view to be treasured.

Realization that so many of my heroes of the celluloid world had spent their play times here, or made films on the spot, gave me a high: Errol Flynn, Humphrey Bogart and Lauren Bacall, for a start.

Next, we were off to Ensenada, Mexico, where the poverty was all too apparent, and where Mariachi bands strutted up and down. In a way it was good to visit and spend a little much-needed money there, and yet sad, because of the scarcity we saw.

Then we sailed away into the low mist that hung over the Pacific and woke up back in LA. Kinda neat—huh!

The non-stop flight home to the UK was unforgettable. From LAX the pilot headed out to sea, where he made a wide swoop; and behold, Los Angeles—from its shoreline to the foothills of the Sierras—with valleys and hillsides bedecked with homes and swimming pools. They all lay before us.

The steady climb into the stratosphere was being made at twilight time, with giant shadows cast by towering ranges everywhere. Textures of red and gold lit up the ancient Western Cordilliera, and then later glorified the outlines of the Rockies—passing slowly and gently below.

This timeless beauty spread out and resplendent in the setting sun was unforgetable. All was dark as we cleared South-East Canada en-route for home; and the fast-flowing jet stream helped us on our way.

2011—From the 'Big Apple' to the James River and Back

Our most recent flight across the ocean that everyone calls a 'pond' was made in September

2011. That itself was a change—our visits have nearly always been in April, or at least springtime.

Touchdown and first abode was Newark, New Jersey. Now, there's something else! The excellent hotel was in the middle of a mixed neighbourhood, but it was near Penn station, which made getting into Penn station, New York, or to Central Point, very easy.

Our mobile phone (the one Americans call a 'cell phone') required a few tweaks, so, we went shopping, just when the whole black population, or so it seemed to us, was going home from work.

We exchanged mutual quizzical looks, ours in reaction to theirs. I think the darting glances were because we didn't appear freaked out in any way. My wife and I are completely colour blind—to us, people are just people—and what's more, a healthy ethnic mix is something quite common in the UK.

In fact the fun and laughter we saw while in the midst of the throng was catching. One guy received a bat in the ear from another because he was blowing a whistle loudly a mere two inches away from his earhole. They gave each other a slap on the arm and laughed.

Trying to look at myself from the American black man's point of view, though, I still don't think it is possible for him—with a mountain of history on his back—to see whites in the same light.

As we continued our peramblation along the streets of Newark the mixture of races became more than exciting. In the phone shop we were looked after (not served, nobody likes that terminology in the USA) by an Italian American, while a Korean worked away near the doorway. Another bloke, from the Middle East, if I remember, could talk for America. I have a smattering of Arabic and it was fun trying it out with him while the phone was being altered.

So what of New York, New York, our next visit? Well, I had seen it in so many movies it was like coming home, and did not disappoint.

It is impossible to escape the ramifications of 9/11, but if any people can do it, then it will be New Yorkers. From the new towers going up beside the big hole in the ground that marks the scene of the atrocity, we joined the throng going down Broadway; then Wall Street, the 'brass bull' and a seat in the pretty little park beside it.

A meal and a chat with an Irish-American barmaid in a typically Irish pub was a highlight. We were even swopping e-mail addresses before leaving.

Onwards to the Battery and its park, to views of the Staten ferry leaving, of Ellis Island and the Statue of Liberty. This made us think of Margaret's grand parents arriving there in 1911.

A bus tour followed: alongside the East River, the Brooklyn Bridge and United Nations building. Onwards to see (among others) the Empire State Building, Trump Towers and 'The Rock'. Mr Trump (who had a Scottish mother, and is busy falling out with people in Aberdeenshire, where he is building *the* golf course) owns several tall buildings in Manhattan. These are pointed out to the traveller who sits on the upper deck of a tour bus, accompanied by jokes at his expense—always something to do with his hair, if I remember right.

Empire State Building from the Rockefeller Centre

The Rockefeller Building, which we ascended later in the week, gave a magnificent panorama of the huge metropolis and beyond, and right slap bang in the middle was The Empire State Building. Central Park was a must see, as was Times Square, where we waved to ourselves on the giant screen set among the neons. While in this colourful wonderland, we paid our due respects to the figurine of Mr George M Cohan.

Times Square

The rendezvous at Madison Gardens with our son, over from Sydney, Australia to be best man at his chum's wedding (to take place in Liberty Field) was a real highlight. We were going to this marvellous event too: to the marriage of a handsome young Chinese man, born and raised in Scotland, who, in Sydney, Australia, met and became betrothed to such a beautiful Korean-American lady, raised in the US.

The wedding, with the Hudson River, Manhattan skyline and the Statue of Liberty as backdrop, beat anything I had ever seen before. The formal procedure was American, but was followed by the families dressed in time-honoured Korean and Chinese costumes performing traditional ceremonies. All this, and a gargantuan feast, songs, speeches and dancing, took place on a fabulous evening.

As night began to fall, and before the twinkling lights came on, we saw a transformation as the great cliff-face of skyscrapers across the Hudson, positively glowed red-gold from the setting sun.

Liberty Field, New Jersey - Manhattan Skyline over the Hudson

A day or two before the wedding, we had moved to Jersey City. Walking the wooden decks that skirt the Hudson we were kept busy counting the number of helicopter flights ferrying tourists the length of the river.

Shopping in the malls was again, *de rigour*; and hairdos were a must; as was ambling around marinas and making friends with New York firemen having a formal re-union. Naturally, photographs were taken, incorporating two 'fellas' dressed in kilts, and sporting tartans that we even recognised. The weather—it was brilliant.

The day following the wedding also turned into an unexpected adventure. Beforehand, we had purchased tickets for the rail journey to Ashland, Virginia, beginning in Philadelphia. We had intended to 'reach into the countryside of New Jersey State, via local railtracks. We were delighted, instead, to be invited to travel to Philly in the car of a fellow-guest, a friend of the bride's father.

He was a real crackerjack, a livewire. Luckily, he had married a lady able to keep up with him and who could provide solace, as and when required. Their house was on the Jersey side of the Delaware, and of course, we had to visit there first.

Following an exceptional meal at a small restaurant that once upon a time had certain—er! shall we say, 'connections', a tour of the city took place, and it was pointed out where to visit the next day. We were then dropped off safely at the door of our hotel. In other words, we received hospitality of the first order from Americans who scarcely knew us. This encapsulates perfectly all I have been trying to say about the ordinary US citizen.

From our hotel we advanced upon 'Rocky's Steps', a short distance away, which were climbed by my son and heir—not me. Photographs were taken; the statue to 'Rocky', just to one side, was examined, as were the other sculptures round about.

We then charged around Philadelphia on a dippy little wooden-seated train-cum-bus to see the sights: from the harbour to the Liberty Bell, and an examination of its famous crack. The old quarter was a revelation; and we saluted the modern metallic sculpture to Edison. The burial plot of the man who was possibly the first 'Philadelphia Lawyer' made me smile. I even ate some pretzels—ugh!

After breakfast next day, it was a matter of boarding the Amtrak train at the magnificent railtrack station, platform five! The inside of this stately building was, literally speaking, sumptious. No wonder it has appeared in so many movies.

Baltimore was a little down the line, then Washington, where, believe it or not, because of ancient agreements, the locomotives had to be changed to journey on into the south.

Fredericksburg came and went, railcars full of noisy, friendly people going home from work; and finally, Ashland, 'Centre of the Universe' as a local wag put it.

We would visit Monticello once more; cross the James River; and together with other places of great interest, visit Williamsburg again and its great college.

Later, we would dine with these, the most hospitable of Americans, together with their chums; truly friendships made in the spirit of 'hands across the sea', a phrase coined by FDR and Churchill between the World Wars.

It was departure time, and as we stood in the little building that lay alongside these tracks running through the middle of town, and which now served as a place to wait for the train, my mind wandered. I could imagine standing quietly beside the rails, around 1865, and in the silence, listening, as is still done today, hearing the rails hum with the wheels of some locomotive while it was still out of sight and being able to tell whether it was approaching, from the north or south.

Upon arrival, it would have evoked shrieks of happiness, or moans of despair, depending on the uniforms worn by the troops arriving, whether they were of the grey or the blue.

I also noted with quiet satisfaction that the rooms in this little house, which had once kept blacks and whites segregated, now served everyone together.

Far too soon, however, we were back in Newark airport and only a matter of hours later, not days, weeks or months, resting in our own home.

Where will it be next? There is little doubt that in the not too distant future the soil of America will bear the imprint of my feet: maybe Wyoming or Seattle and Portland, or New England and hopefully Texas. So, look out for us on the trail, y'all...

◆◆◆

◆◆◆

Well done folks if you have read to here—you're made of stern stuff!

Being so tough, you might have the nerve to leave a review on the Amazon website.

Many thanks.

About the author

I write History, Fiction, Non-Fiction (stories, essays and poetry).

The historical material comes in book and e-book form; all the rest is digital and to be found on Amazon.

You can contact me about my books or anything else at: http://georgemcgilvary.com/